I WANT TO KNOW

Was King Arthur Real?

Portia Summers

Enslow Publishing
101 W. 23rd Street
Suite 240
New York, NY 10011
USA

enslow.com

Published in 2018 by Enslow Publishing, LLC.
101 W. 23rd Street, Suite 240, New York, NY 10011

Library of Congress Cataloging-in-Publication Data

Names: Summers, Portia, author.
Title: Was King Arthur real? / Portia Summers.
Description: New York, NY : Enslow Publishing, 2018. | Series: I want to know
 | Includes bibliographical references and index. | Audience: Grade 3 to 5.
Identifiers: LCCN 2017017707| ISBN 9780766092006 (library bound) | ISBN
 9780766093805 (pbk.) | ISBN 9780766093812 (6 pack)
Subjects: LCSH: Arthur, King—Juvenile literature. | Britons—Kings and rulers—
 Juvenile literature. | Great Britain—History—To 1066—Juvenile literature.
Classification: LCC DA152.5.A7 S9 2018 | DDC 942.01/4—dc23
LC record available at https://lccn.loc.gov/2017017707

Printed in China

To Our Readers: We have done our best to make sure all websites in this book were
active and appropriate when we went to press. However, the author and the publisher
have no control over and assume no liability for the material available on those websites
or on any websites they may link to. Any comments or suggestions can be sent by email
to customerservice@enslow.com.

Photo Credits: Cover Fer Gregory/Shutterstock.com; pp. 3, 17 (statue) Marco Nijland/
Shutterstock.com; p. 5 Hilary Morgan/Alamy Stock Photo; p. 7 Culture Club/Hulton
Archive/Getty Images; p. 9 DEA Picture Library/De Agostini/Getty Images; p. 11 DEA/J.
E. Bulloz/De Agostini/Getty Images; p. 14 Private Collection/Bridgeman Images; p. 15
Commission Air/Alamy Stock Photo; p. 16 Jean Williamson/LOOP Images/Corbis Docu-
mentary/Getty Images; p. 17 (castle ruins) stocker1970/Shutterstock.com; p. 18 schistra/
Shutterstock.com; p. 20 Everett Collection, Inc./Alamy Stock Photo; p. 22 Heritage Imag-
es/Hulton Fine Art Collection/Getty Images; p. 24 Interim Archives/Archive Photos/Getty
Images; p. 26 (top) Ivy Close Images/Alamy Stock; p. 26 (bottom) Leemage/Universal
Images Group/Getty Images; p. 27 Charles Phelps Cushing/ClassicStock/Archive Photos/
Getty Images.

Contents

Chapter 1

· · · · · · · · · · ·

Once Upon a Time

Once upon a time, in a land far, far away, there lived a legendary king named Arthur. He was handsome, wise, and just. He was married to a beautiful queen, Guinevere, and led a group of **chivalrous** knights who went on **quests** to save people from dangerous monsters. Arthur had the help of a wise magician named Merlin, and together they created a beautiful and prosperous **utopia** called Camelot.

King Arthur was legendary for his leadership and his adventures. But was King Arthur real? Or was he the stuff of legend?

King Arthur and Queen Guinevere wed. King Arthur and his court inspired many stories and ideas that people hold about medieval life.

The Story of King Arthur

The legend of King Arthur is an **epic** tale of adventure. There are different versions of Arthur's beginnings. Some stories say he was raised by his father, Uther Pendragon, a king, and inherited his throne. More modern tellings of the story say he was raised by a country knight, never knowing of his **parentage**. In these stories, when Arthur was a young man, he pulled a sword called Excalibur from a stone. He became the king of all of Britain, which was filled with war, poverty, and struggling people.

The young King Arthur was tested many times. But his most famous feat was his defeat of the Saxon invaders (from modern-day Germany). Arthur made Britain a free kingdom under his rule. He went on to build Camelot, a walled city where the citizens were safe and well fed.

One of the most famous stories of King Arthur was when he pulled Excalibur from the stone and became king of England.

Knights of the Round Table

King Arthur was a fair and just ruler, but he did not rule Camelot alone. Besides Merlin and Guinevere, Arthur also had his loyal knights who were known for being pure of heart and for doing good deeds throughout the kingdom.

Equality for all his people was important to Arthur. When he created the place to meet with his knights, he built a large, round table. Because of the shape of the table, there was no head of the table, which meant that everyone who sat around it was equal.

King Arthur and his knights often went on quests to kill dragons and other beasts and overthrow lords who didn't treat their people fairly. These knights also helped Arthur on the greatest quest of his life: to find the Holy Grail. The Holy Grail is the cup that Jesus drank from on the night of the Last Supper. It is considered a sacred **relic** by Christians. According to legend, Saint Joseph of Arimathea brought the Grail to Britain.

Over many years, King Arthur and his knights crossed all of Britain in search of the Grail. Sir Percival found a run-down castle deep in the woods, but he did not know that was where the Grail was located. It was Lancelot's son, Galahad, who laid eyes on the Grail. While kneeling in prayer,

Knights Galahad, Percival, and Bohors kneel before the Holy Grail.

both Galahad and the Grail ascended into Heaven as Arthur watched.

The Death of King Arthur

Arthur returned to Camelot and discovered that his wife, Guinevere, had fallen in love with Lancelot, his most trusted knight. In anger, Arthur banished Guinevere from Camelot. But the people of Camelot didn't agree with

The Most Famous Knights

There were many stories told about the adventures of King Arthur's knights. Here are a few of the most famous knights of the Round Table *(right)*:

Sir Kay—one of the earliest characters associated with Arthur; his foster brother

Lancelot—Arthur's best friend and the knight who betrays Arthur by falling in love with Guinevere, which causes a civil war and the eventual death of Arthur

Mordred—possibly Arthur's son by Queen Morgause; eventually betrays King Arthur and kills him on the battlefield

Percival—a pure and honest knight who helps Arthur on his quest for the Holy Grail

Sir Ector—the country knight who fostered Arthur when he was a young boy

Galahad—Lancelot's son, who helps King Arthur on his quest for the Holy Grail

Gawain—Arthur's nephew, called one of the greatest knights of the Round Table

Tristan—one of Arthur's knights; fell in love with the Irish princess Iseult and inspired his own romantic legend

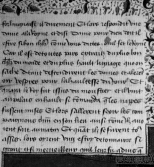

Arthur's decision to banish the queen. And many people outside of Camelot didn't agree with Arthur's decision to keep Britain free.

And so a civil war began. After years of epic battles and adventures, Arthur was old. He depended on his knights. During the Battle of Camlann, one of his knights, Mordred, turned on Arthur and stabbed him with his sword. As the battle raged around him, Arthur died, and Britain was never the same again.

Legend says that Arthur was buried in the mythical island of Avalon, which is guarded by ancient priestesses. It states that one day, Arthur will return when Britain most needs a wise and just ruler to unite them all.

Chapter 2

· · · · · · · · · · ·

Camelot

Many historians have searched for the legendary Camelot. While many believe Camelot was never a real city, there are many places all over the United Kingdom that have been linked to the legend of King Arthur.

Real-Life Castles

Castles are an important part of the Arthur legend. The idea of castles often brings up images of great stone towers and large throne rooms. But in fact, many castles were fortresses, designed to protect from invaders.

Many of the places that were mentioned in the writings about King Arthur were real. Caerleon, South

King Arthur united a very divided England. Before his reign, large sections of the nation were ruled by separate kings.

Wales, was a Roman fortress during the fifth and sixth centuries. It was one of the places where the Britons fought against real-life Saxon invaders.

Cadbury Castle

Another castle that could have been the basis of Camelot is Cadbury Castle in Somerset, England. Cadbury was a hilltop fortress that once housed a great room most likely used for meetings between leaders. Cadbury is located near Glastonbury Tor, a hill shrouded in mystery and legend. A causeway, known as King Arthur's Hunting Track, connects the two sites. According to legend, there is a cave in Cadbury Hill where Arthur and his knights lie asleep until England needs them again.

This is an aerial view of Cadbury Castle in Somerset, one of the many places believed to have been the possible location of Camelot.

Glastonbury Abbey

Glastonbury Abbey is in Somerset, England. The ancient cemetery there is said to hold the remains of many great kings and saints. In 1184 a fire burned a great deal of the church. Soon thereafter, it was claimed that the tomb of Arthur and

Glastonbury Abbey, the legendary burial site of Arthur and Guinevere

Guinevere was discovered in a part of the abbey that had been revealed in the fire. A cross hung above the hidden tomb that read *"Hic jacet sepultus inclitus rex Arthurus in insula Avalonia,"* or "Here lies interred the famous King Arthur on the Isle of Avalon."

Today many historians believe that the tomb and the cross were very good fakes. They were designed to inspire people to donate to the rebuilding of the church.

However, there are those who still visit the ruins of Glastonbury Abbey to see the supposed grave of King Arthur and Guinevere.

Tintagel

Tintagel Castle in Cornwall, England, is another castle that could be the legendary Camelot. Some legends state that it was the place of Arthur's birth.

Tintagel Castle is one of the many places mentioned in Arthurian legend that really exists. It holds a nine-foot statue of King Arthur (*inset*).

A Real Round Table?

There is an artifact in Hampshire, England, known as the Winchester Round Table (*right*). This round tabletop has the names of Arthur's knights carved into its sides. Although it is not the original Round Table of legend, it is what the table of Camelot may have looked like if it were real.

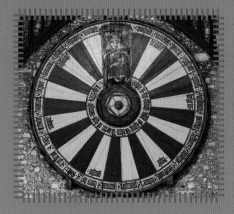

However, the castle is not old enough to have been Camelot. Archeologists have dated the building of the castle to the 1100s. But there are many artifacts that have been unearthed in the area that are far older.

There are many other real places in the stories of King Arthur. Winchester Castle, where the Winchester Round Table hangs, has also been said to be the legendary castle at Camelot. London was also mentioned in the tales, as are the towns of Carlisle, Carhaix, Cardigan, and Quimper. Some historians think that the mystical isle of Avalon may actually be the town of Avallon in France.

Chapter 3

· · · · · · · · · · ·

Real-Life Heroes

Although the story of King Arthur is very famous, was he a real king? Many historians think that King Arthur was, in fact, a **folk hero**, or a combination of many great warriors throughout British history. Some think the story of Arthur is actually based on a Roman warrior who fought in Britain against the Picts and the Saxons. Other historians think that the legend of Arthur may be based on the story of a long-lost Celtic **deity**, or god. And still more do think that Arthur was based on any number of British warriors.

The Legend Lives On

The story of King Arthur has been told by poets and authors for centuries in many languages, including Latin, French, German, Greek, Italian, Hebrew, Norse, and, of course, English. It continues to inspire novelists and filmmakers today. Here are some of the most famous writings, films, and television shows about King Arthur:

Books

A Connecticut Yankee in King Arthur's Court by Mark Twain (1889)

Merlin's Godson by H. Warner Munn (1936)

King Arthur and His Knights of the Round Table by Roger Lancelyn Green (1953)

The Once and Future King by T. H. White (1958)

The Mists of Avalon by Marion Zimmer Bradley (1983)

Movies and TV Shows

The Sword and the Stone (1963)

Monty Python and the Holy Grail (1975)

A Kid in King Arthur's Court (1995)

Merlin (BBC series, 2008–2012)

The Sorcerer's Apprentice (2010)

King Arthur: Legend of the Sword (2017)

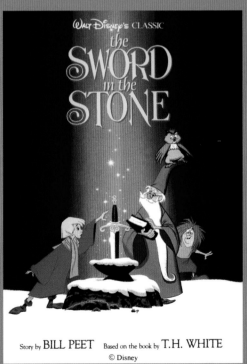

WALT DISNEY'S CLASSIC
the SWORD in the STONE

Story by BILL PEET   Based on the book by T.H. WHITE
© Disney

Historians place the story of Arthur in the fifth or sixth century, at a time when the Roman Empire was collapsing and pulling its troops out of the British Isles. As the legend of Arthur states, the people of Britain were threatened by invading Saxons. It is true that there were many battles fought between the Britons and the Saxons. Yet it is unlikely that one man defeated nine hundred men in battle by himself, as is said of King Arthur in *Historia Brittonum*. But people have turned to the legend during many times of trouble throughout British history in order to give them hope.

Lucius Artorius Castus

Lucius Artorius Castus was a real-life war hero who some historians think may have been the inspiration for Arthur. Not only is Artorius the Latin translation of "Arthur," but Lucius Artorius was a Roman warrior who lived and fought in Britain during the second and third centuries. Lucius

Roman soldiers rest along Hadrian's Wall. Many Roman officers were sent to the British Isles during the reign of the Roman Empire.

Artorius fought near Hadrian's Wall, which was built to keep the people of Britain safe from invading Saxons. It is also said that his **standard**, or symbol, was a red dragon. Arthur's symbol is often a red dragon, too (his father was Uther Pendragon, after all). Lucius Artorius is said to have battled against the Samaritans in his early career. The Samaritans loved their swords, and spent many hours sharpening and cleaning them. At the time, the best way to do that was by using a stone. Perhaps this was the beginning of the legend of the sword in the stone.

Riothamus

Another Roman officer who may have inspired the legend of King Arthur was Riothamus. He lived in the late fifth century and was sent to help the Britons defeat Saxon invaders. He went to Gaul (in modern-day France) to help defeat the Visigoths. Arthur was said to have traveled to Gaul twice, once to help the Romans and once to stop a civil war. Riothamus did both of these things. But on his last trip to Gaul, one of his captains told

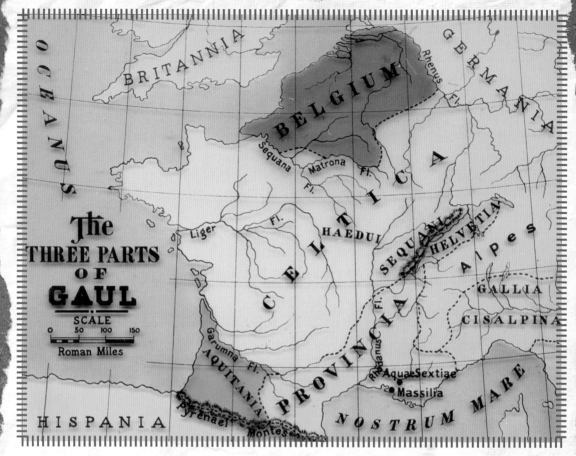

The map text includes: OCEANUS, BRITANNIA, GERMANIA, BELGIUM, Rhenus Fl., Sequana Fl., Matrona Fl., CELTICA, Liger Fl., HAEDUI, SEQUANI, HELVETIA, Alpes, GALLIA CISALPINA, PROVINCIA, Rhodanus Fl., AquaeSextiae, Massilia, NOSTRUM MARE, AQUITANIA, Garumna Fl., Pyrenaei Montes, HISPANIA

The
THREE PARTS
O F
GAUL
SCALE
0 50 100 150
Roman Miles

Gaul was the country just to the south of Britain. In Julius Caesar's time, Gaul was divided into three parts: Belgica, Celtica, and Aquitania.

the enemy the location of his army, much like Mordred did to Arthur in his final battle. Riothamus died in Gaul similarly to how Arthur was said to have died.

Chapter 4

· · · · · · · · · ·

The Man, the Myth, the Legend

Arthur may or may not have been a real person, but he is a true hero. A hero, after all, is someone who gives people hope in times of trouble. The story of Arthur has been told over and over again. It continues to inspire people to hope again for a time when people were brave and true, when magic was everywhere, and when there was peace around the world.

Imagine That!

Although the story of King Arthur was very popular in the Middle Ages, it became less popular over time. However, the **Victorian** poet Alfred, Lord Tennyson wrote several poems based on the legend of King Arthur and made the story popular again.

The Power of Myth

There is no doubt that the legend of King Arthur is still a story that holds power over readers. The legendary battles and characters, as well as the chivalry and good morals that Arthur is said to have had, are told and retold.

Perhaps what makes the story so powerful is that there seems to be evidence that it could be true. During the Middle Ages, there were many kings and warlords in Europe. The countryside had many castles and

King Arthur (*left*) and Merlin

A prince collects taxes from his subjects in medieval Europe.

Code of Chivalry

Knights of the Middle Ages followed a code of chivalry. The code began during the Crusades (1095–1291), when soldiers who fought in Jerusalem were taught to behave according to certain rules. Much like the Christian priests who led the soldiers during the Crusades, knights had ten commandments by which they had to live:

1. To believe all that the church teaches and follow all its rules.

2. To defend the church.

3. To respect those weaker than them and defend them.

4. To love the country in which they were born.

5. To not cower before their enemies.

6. To fight against their enemies without stopping and without mercy.

7. To completely and thoroughly perform their knightly duties, as long as these duties didn't go against the laws of God.

8. To never lie and to keep their promises.

9. To be generous to everyone.

10. To be everywhere and always the champion of the right and the good against injustice and evil.

knights. Some were good and just. Others were ruthless and cruel. The people who lived under cruel leaders longed for fair ones. The idea of a fair and wise ruler like Arthur would have been a very popular one. Including magic and religion simply made the story much more interesting.

An Everlasting Story

King Arthur may have been a real person, but his feats have most certainly been exaggerated over the centuries. Archeologists and historians are still looking for proof of King Arthur, his brave knights, and his beautiful kingdom. It is possible that the truth of King Arthur is still out there, waiting to be unburied. Or it is possible that King Arthur is just a really good story that continues to inspire hope. Either way, the legend of King Arthur will certainly continue to be told for more centuries to come.

Words to Know

chivalrous Living by a code of honor and bravery.

deity A god.

epic Describing a grand adventure; heroic; extraordinary.

folk hero A person, real or fictional, looked up to by people of a particular culture or place.

Midsummer's Eve A holiday in June that celebrates the longest day of the year in the Northern Hemisphere.

parentage Family history.

quest A journey in which a person searches for something or someone.

relic An object that is old and historically important.

standard A personal symbol used by a king.

utopia A perfect society.

Victorian Living in the time of Queen Victoria, the ruler of the United Kingdom (1837–1901).

Further Reading

Books

Hunter, Nick. *Did King Arthur Exist?* London: Raintree, 2016.

Lanier, Sidney. *King Arthur and the Knights of the Round Table.* New York, NY: Racehorse for Young Readers, 2017.

Saxena, Shalini. *The Legend of King Arthur.* New York, NY: Gareth Stevens Publishing, 2015.

White, T. H. *The Once and Future King.* New York, NY: Penguin Classics, 2009.

Websites

Caerleon.net

www.caerleon.net/history/arthur/index.htm

Dive deeper into the connection between King Arthur and the Welsh town of Caerleon.

History for Kids

www.historyforkids.net/king-arthur.html

Read more about King Arthur and the Middle Ages.

PBS.org

www.pbs.org/mythsandheroes/myths_four_arthur.html

Learn more about King Arthur and the real-life people, places, and events behind the myth.

Index